"By following the ideas in this book, Rich Rozman showed us how to get the right protection at one-half the cost."

Matt and Kathy Fadorsen, Owners
Arabica Coffee Houses

"The ideas in his book are why my business insurance works so well."

Nate Johnson, President
Johnson's Landscaping, Inc.

"I recommend you talk to Rich about your insurance needs. You will probably need to invest about an hour of your time and he will do all the work from there."

Christopher O'Donnell
Owens Flooring Company

"…there are significant monetary savings over our old plan…we do not worry about not having the correct type or right amount of protection."

Terry and Sally Phillips
Suburban Machinery, Inc.

101 Business Insurance Mistakes You DON'T Want To Make!

Rich Rozman

First Edition 2010

To my family and loved ones, who have shown me the greatest examples of love and life.

A special gratitude is owed to the late John Thompson of the Beacon Insurance Company of America. John was a beacon, professional and personal, to all who knew him.

Contents

Introduction

This book WILL save you time and, possibly, your company.

This book WILL NOT make you an insurance expert.

I haven't found a good, basic, easy-to-read, business insurance book for the beginning entrepreneur, seasoned contractor, or experienced manufacturer. So I wrote one.

This book will fill the "insurance information gap" for you. It may not answer every question you have, but if you read this book, consider the risks facing your company and manage the risks discussed in this book, you will be far, far ahead of your peers and competition.

Here are a few guiding "gems" for your consideration:

> Don't risk a lot to save a little.

> You don't know what will happen, when it will happen, or to what extent it will happen. People that think they do are fooling themselves.

Don't even think there is such a thing as "free insurance". It costs you, somewhere or sometime.

Nobody knows everything. Not in insurance, anyway!

Sometimes, you just need to ask the right questions. This book will give you some of the ideas and vocabulary to do that. If you don't find what you are looking for in this book, contact me and suggest that I add it to the next edition.

Using just one of the time-tested ideas in this book could save you thousands or millions of dollars, or even your company.

The information is presented in small paragraphs or "bursts", so you don't have to churn through huge volumes of material to find your answer. Important words are "**bolded**" so they are easier to find.

This book is mostly my opinion, acquired over 30 years in the insurance industry. **Always, always, always** get the opinion of competent professionals who know (or are willing to learn about) your <u>specific</u> situation.

If you have additional questions or problems, you should contact your agent or broker. If you still can't get an understandable answer, contact me:

Rich Rozman (the Insurance Guy, to many)
P.O. Box 1776
Willoughby OH 44094-1776
<u>rrozman@seibertkeck.com</u>

Five Sources of Risk

Nature
(windstorms, lightning, earthquake, flood)

Operations
(fire, vehicle collision, theft)

Customers
(product liability, slips & falls, E&O issues)

Employees
(workers compensation, embezzlements, employment practices)

Owners, Officers, & Managers
(D&O issues, employer liability issues, employment practices)

The following pages explain how modern business or commercial insurance can reduce the ultimate risk from these Five Sources.

Reviewing and refocusing on these Five Sources from time to time will help you assess various threats to the financial well being of your business.

You need to know that your personal insurance (homeowners, auto, and personal umbrella) is NOT a substitute for commercial insurance. Most parts are mutually exclusive of each other.

Property Insurance
Don'ts and Do's

1. Don't insure what you would not claim.

2. Don't insure what you would fix yourself.

3. Don't insure if the insurance company gives you a good discount for retaining the risk (deductible credits).

4. Do insure the risk that would really hurt, be financially difficult or disastrous to your company (catastrophic loss).

5. Do insure your **manufacturing equipment** properly. In a word: Overinsure. How do you know the correct amount?

   If it's new or a current production machine, it's easy; just check with the manufacturer.

   If it's older, unique, custom-made and critical to your process, it's tougher, but here are a couple of ideas:

   Method #1: Take the original cost, inflate it to today's dollar and add a reasonable margin for error.

Method #2: If there is a "used" market, check those prices and add a generous reconditioning margin.

Method #3: Manufacture it "on paper." Break it down, piece by piece to get the component costs to manufacture each (you may need a consulting engineer to help), add the cost to assemble, test run and then tune up. You <u>need</u> to know these costs. Someone said, "Ignorance isn't bliss, it's oblivion."

6. Do insure your buildings properly. If they're new, it's easy. If you would rebuild or replace, use the **Replacement Cost** valuation and insure to the full value (more on this later).

   If you would not rebuild or replace the current structure, consider using a **depreciated basis** or "**Actual Cash Value**" valuation. This could reduce your insurance basis by as much as 50%. The rates don't change, only the basis. Be aware, though, when a claim is paid, it can be reduced by the depreciation rate, too.

   Give this idea some thought: One of my clients, Dan, was convinced he couldn't insure his building. Dan thought the premium was too large and not in the realm of financial possibility for his company. They thought they "would just take their chances" and hope.

   We used an outrageously large deductible (relative to the value of the building), saved a lot of premium and were able to insure his entire building. The large deductible drove the premium way down, but then Dan was able to insure for the really big, catastrophic, or total loss.

Instead of risking the loss of everything because he thought the insurance was not affordable, we determined the worst "hit" he could assume and decided to take it off the front end. Keep in mind, though, Dan is on EVERY risk for that large deductible (but he was at risk for everything before).

7. Insurance companies call it a "provision. I call it a "hidden time bomb." Its name is **Coinsurance**.

You pay for your insurance with your hard-earned money. You deserve great advice and fair claims settlement. But, if you underinsure to save premium (risking a lot to save a little), or are advised to underinsure by your broker (so they make the premium look less in order to make a sale?), you will not receive a full claim settlement. You didn't spend your money to get half a claim settlement, but it could happen!

The coinsurance penalty works like this: You are paid in the same proportion as you insure your property. Insure half, get paid half a claim. It may be manageable if it's a $10,000 claim, but what if it's a $200,000 or $1,000,000 claim? You could create a very bad situation for your company. Most insurance companies give you some amount of margin of error (10% or 20%), but you pay more for that margin. It's better to remove the Coinsurance Penalty altogether, and have the insurance company agree on the values. Hence the term, "**Agreed Value**." It's a good idea. It's a good endorsement.

If an advisor, broker, CPA, attorney, etc., suggests underinsuring your property, be sure to have them put their "professional advice" in writing, on their firm's stationery, and sign it. You'll need it for evidence in the lawsuit when you sue them for the amount the insurance company won't pay…

8. If your equipment is old, you know how to rebuild or refurbish it, or there is a lot of the same type of equipment on the used market, you could save a lost of money by insuring it on a **"Functional Replacement Cost"** basis. This basis changes the valuation concept from the Replacement Cost concept of "new for old, like kind and quality", to "similar function." This change of valuation could reduce your insurance basis by 50% to 70%, sometimes. Ask your broker!

   The same goes for your building. If you are using only a fraction of it, and would not replace it, why insure it? If the difference between what you "have" and what you "use" is greater than 35%, you should investigate this option with your broker.

9. Don't assume that if it is a **"building item"** or "building feature" that it is automatically covered. Usually, coverage "stops at grade." Below grade items such as flues, piping, underground wiring, pre-treatment plants, and special foundations may not be insured. They may not be so easily damaged, but you can still suffer a loss if they cannot be reused. (See #21)

10. Don't assume **FLOOD** is covered. Everyplace in the U.S. is in a "flood zone." It's up to you to ask your broker to check with the National Flood Insurance Program (part of FEMA) for your flood zone description. Occasionally, the insurance company "gives" you some flood coverage, but it's rarely enough when you need it.

11. Don't believe **"water damage"** is automatically covered, either. In a "standard" policy, three out of six common causes

of loss by water are specifically excluded: Sewer or drain backup, hydrostatic pressure against a foundation wall, water coming in through an unbroken building surface (you left the window open…). Many companies let you "buy back" the sewer or drain backup hazard, but only for a limited amount of damage. Ask your broker!

12. One type of water damage that is specifically EXCLUDED is **"surface water"**. Some might call it "run off" and it is water that is flowing across the ground, pavement, or other surface. It's not "rising water", like a river overflowing its banks; it's actually "descending water", headed for a lower elevation. It's just unfortunate that you're in the way…

13. There are several types of "property" that insurance doesn't cover as "property." One is Boilers and Machinery. Today, the category can include computer networks, fiber optic systems, elevators, and HVAC equipment. The list seems to grow every day. **"Equipment Breakdown"** or "Mechanical Breakdown" pays for damage (subject to deductibles or waiting periods) when the equipment is damaged from a cause ("accident") that damages the machinery, including from within the machinery. It can be just as devastating as a fire or lightning strike, but it is not "property" coverage. Ask your broker about it – most insurance companies now have very reasonably priced coverage for this type of loss.

14. If you make a physical product, don't assume your **"profit"** will be included in a loss settlement. It is generally NOT part of the value of the object if you still own it. Protect yourself a little more by asking for a quote on a **"Manufacturer's Selling Price"** endorsement. It probably won't be as expensive as you think.

15. Don't assume "**Blanket Property Insurance**" gives you the best protection. "Blankets" are most useful when there are multiple locations (dispersion of risk) or inventory that may move from one insured location to another. "Blankets" are worse when they are used for only one location and to reduce the overall insurance by combining both building and business personal property into one lower limit of insurance.

    This false economy (it can lower premiums, if you lower your limit of protection) does not solve the following problems:

    You retain the Coinsurance Penalty
    You have insufficient insurance in the case of a total loss
    You create a "lazy mind" attitude for valuations and determining amounts of insurance.

16. When comparing two or more policies, remember that they will NEVER be identical. Be sure YOU specify what coverage and for what amounts are important or critical to you. Don't get misled into making your decision based on some minor difference that doesn't mean anything in YOUR practical world.

17. Don't assume your property insurance is intact if your building has been **vacant** for more than 60 days. The "standard adjustment" for a vacant building is that there is NO COVERAGE for six (6) common types of claims and only 85% for some of the others; the valuation basis changes to "Actual Cash Value" (depreciated, not replacement cost) and all the other exclusions still apply. NOT GOOD for YOU. Get a "Vacancy Permit" whenever possible and be aware of this

potentially huge problem and watch the occupancy percentage that causes this drastic decrease in protection.

18. Don't assume your policy covers every kind of loss. The Property Section in this book uses the concepts found in the "Special Causes of Loss" property form. It's more expensive than just "fire insurance", but it protects you from many more types of losses. And since you aren't choosing what kind of loss you will have (unless you're an arsonist), protection against the greatest number of causes of loss make sense.

The cost to improve or increase the causes of loss looks something like this:

Basic	45%	or	100%
Broad	70%	or	164%
Special	100%	or	243%

The above table isn't exact, and it will vary for different types of construction, and whether you're insuring a building or contents, but it approximates the cost of expanding your protection.

19. Don't assume that the **building replacement cost estimate** (BRCE) for your building is accurate or is estimating what will be covered by your policy. One of the very first BRCE that I received from an underwriter who was using a "state of the art" estimating system was wrong. He explained how the system was continually updated for trends in building costs, adjusted by building ages, 9-digit zipcodes, specific neighborhood information, etc. After listening to him defend his "state of the art" system, I had to explain to him that the address was wrong and the estimate was for a different building…Most BRCE

include sub-grade features that most insurance policies do not cover. You can avoid this by carefully reviewing the BRCE or by adding special endorsements to cover below grade building features such as foundations, piping, flues, etc.

20. Don't assume that **artwork, antiques, manuscripts** or other property that has special values due to their uniqueness will be adequately protected by your property policy. You should have special appraisals to support your valuation. You should also use a "stated value" class for the property or insure it on an Inland Marine type policy with a "stated value." Some policies afford the best protection when you use an "agreed value." You must read the fine print and understand the valuation method to know how your specific policy will respond.

Crime Insurance Don'ts and Do's

1. Don't assume money, negotiable instruments, securities are considered "property" in the insurance world. There is a special category called "Crime" to handle these intrinsically high value items of commerce.

2. **Money (cash)** has very limited protection, if at all, in most policies. Coverage is usually very specific and restricted (inside vs. outside). It's also expensive. Don't assume you have protection against loss of money in your policy. See it. Ask your broker.

3. The most comprehensive cash money protection (at the time of this printing) would be "**Money & Securities**", sometimes called Form C. There are often different amounts of protection for money inside your building and away from your building. Always ask for this coverage because, by itself, it is the broadest coverage, offering protection from the greatest number of types of loss (theft, disappearance or destruction).

4. The better description or coverage type for protection against employees stealing from your company is "**Employee Theft**"

not "Employee Dishonesty." It's a technical difference, but one that might result in a loss being paid or not.

5. Don't assume Crime coverage is for money only. Almost any company property is subject to possible **theft, conversion, or embezzlement**. Raw materials, stock, finished inventory, tools, office equipment or supplies all "walk" or can "develop legs." It can add up to a lot of money, very quickly, especially if the employee has a large need to fill and the proper controls are not in place. Consider all the possibilities.

6. In some instances, you can even obtain coverage if your **employee steals from your customers**. It's a special type of insurance, but it does exist. Ask your broker.

7. You need special protection for loss through the Internet or electronic funds transfer. **Computer fraud** and other "hacker" activity create the need for these types of protection. If you ever have a lot of money "in play" on the Internet, you need this protection.

8. The best protection is **prevention. For employee theft** issues that means: good banking, audit, and security controls. Your CPA should be able to suggest at least a rudimentary program for a "first line of defense" against these types of losses. Your security advisors may even suggest card keys, closed circuit television (CCTV) monitoring, etc. Ask your broker to check with your insurance company's loss control department. They may be of help, too.

9. Hint: Know your **operating ratios**. Not only are they the guides to profitability, but to your company's financial security, as well. Unusual changes in revenues to material

cost, shipping weight to invoice values, labor cost to production, etc. are security metrics, too. Of course, spikes or other changes in the inputs or ratios when specific employees are not present, reveal much information.

Liability Insurance Don'ts and Do's

1. Don't assume EVERYTHING from your business activity goes into your **liability basis for premium calculation purposes**. For instance, if you are "Payroll" based, office or overtime should not count. If you are "Sales" based, sales tax, returns, and freight should NOT be included. (You probably just saved the price of this book hundreds of times over with that one!)

2. One of the easiest (and least expensive) ways to get additional general liability protection is to add endorsements for "Aggregate Limits per Location" and "Aggregate Limits per Project" if either would apply to your operations. Do you have **multiple locations**? Offsite projects? This endorsement could have a major beneficial effect for you.

3. Another coverage "multiplier" for your protection is an **aggregate limit of insurance** that is a two or three times multiple of your "per occurrence" limit of insurance. Modifying the aggregate limit will give you a "reserve" to fall back on if you have one or more severe claims in a policy year. Think about this: if you had enough severe losses to exhaust your limit of insurance, what insurance company would want

to insure you? Build this protection into your program <u>at the start.</u>

4. **Certificates of Liability Insurance** should be produced for you at no charge by your broker (it's a service industry, isn't it?). If a customer or lessor requires you to name them as an "additional insured" it's usually no big deal. If fifty customers require it, it becomes a big deal unless you have a "blanket additional insured" provision in your policy. You should have this endorsement and it's usually a more economical way for you to satisfy your customers' insurance requirements.

5. Endorsements are sometimes available for "**Waiver of Subrogation**" or "Waiver of Right of Recovery", too. Sometimes "**primary and non-contributory**" wording is specified. It's more and more common for companies to try to shift liability away from themselves or to try to have others' insurance available to pay for a big loss if it happens. Municipalities, sellers, and buyers all try to do it. Check with your broker. The broker must follow the insurance company's directions and offer only what the insurance company approves, but these endorsements are used with increasing frequency.

6. Don't assume that a request for being named on your policy as an "additional insured" is rational. A rule of thumb is that the naming of an additional insured "flows in the opposite direction of the money". This means that it is logical for a customer or vendor (someone to whom you sell your product) to request being named as an additional insured on your policy, but not your supplier (someone who sells you material). Having said that, it is common for a grantor of a franchise to request it.

7. If you are requesting the certificate or are the **certificate holder**, do not accept a blank copy or one that is not completed and signed by the agent. Only agents and insurance companies can issue certificates. It's <u>not</u> a do-it-yourself process. If an agent or company won't issue it, there is probably a good reason – like a policy lapse or non-renewal occurred.

8. Don't assume all products are easily insured. **Product Liability** for medical devices, implants, pharmaceuticals, aircraft parts, industrial, or construction machinery all give underwriters headaches. But, that's what they're paid for, right? "High Risk" products require "High Risk" product liability insurance and it can be very expensive. Give your broker and the underwriters the facts (read: truth) and let them make their best decision. "Fudging" what you do only creates the potential for declined claims and fraud lawsuits.

9. Don't assume your General Liability Products coverage will provide you with **Product Recall Expense**. Don't assume it is a simple and inexpensive task to recall lots of product, either. Some "standard" insurance companies now offer it, but you will probably need to investigate the Excess & Surplus markets (specialty and high risk) for the larger amounts of protection.

10. Don't assume your policy has any **pollution coverage**. If it does, it probably isn't much. As one environmental specialist told me, "Given the right circumstances, even deionized water could be considered a pollutant." If your manufacturing process uses liquids or gases, investigate this important insurance protection with your broker.

11. Don't assume that if you include or increase a **deductible on your General Liability** coverage, your premium will change

significantly. Much of the premium may depend on whether "frequency" or "severity" governs the underwriting decision and premium rate. If it's severity, there may be no change at all because the insurance company believes any claim will become large very quickly and any deductible would be too small to offset much of the claim. If it's frequency that influences the underwriting decision, you may be required to accept a deductible.

12. Usually a **"per occurrence" deductible** is preferable to **a "per claim" deductible**. The difference is best illustrated by a claim involving some type of damage caused by a contractor overspraying some area and damaging several automobiles. A per occurrence deductible would result in one deductible for the incident. A per claim deductible would result in one deductible for <u>each</u> automobile damaged.

13. Don't assume your policy has protection for **"cyberliability"** issues. This is a very new area for insurers and most will avoid it. These types of losses could be for corruption or theft of data for which you have a responsibility. Examples may be employee personal data, customer's banking information, etc. The 2009 cost for damages per compromised record or account was approximately $180. This can add up very quickly and have a very damaging ripple effect throughout an organization.

14. By the way, "importing" isn't "distributing," "roofing" isn't "carpentry" and "machine rebuilding" isn't "machine shop." Don't assume your application accurately describes your business. You signed it. You should have read it. If it isn't accurate, you may have created a reason for a claim denial. Review your business activities with your broker.

15. Don't assume your General Liability policy will protect you if an **employee claims harassment, discrimination, or violation of labor laws or regulations**. The only policy that will respond for you in such a situation is one that provides protection for "**employment practices**." Fortunately, this type of insurance is increasingly more common and many insurance companies offer loss control assistance to help you avoid claims. You guessed it, ask your broker!

16. Don't assume all will go well with **contractors** you hire to work on your premises or property. Always get a certificate of insurance naming you as certificate holder. Always get a copy of the contractor's workers compensation certificate. Always be sure they are properly licensed for what they do.

17. Some insurance companies and, more frequently, those that operate in what is called the "excess and surplus market" often put exclusions for **specific or designated** products, locations, work performed, or professional services in their policies. If you see one of these exclusions, know that the insurance company has no intention of providing coverage for that particular type of loss.

18. Don't leave yourself exposed to employee lawsuits. Remove the **Fellow Employee Exclusion** so your policy, not your company, will pay if one employee sues another for bodily injury damage.

Professional Liability Insurance Don'ts and Do's

1. If you are selling advice, **consulting,** offering professional opinions, designing or troubleshooting for a fee, don't assume your General Liability policy will protect you. Consultants, engineers, architects, accountants, physicians, attorneys all need **professional liability protection**. It's often the most important protection in the insurance program. It's often the most expensive, too.

2. Many **Directors and Officers** are poorly protected in their company's insurance programs. If, <u>while performing his duties,</u> a maintenance person accidentally throws a stone with a lawn mower, hurts someone and is sued as a result, he is protected by the General Liability policy. If a director, officer, or manager, <u>while performing her duties,</u> is alleged to have made the wrong decision and someone feels they have been hurt by the decision, the officer or board member is often left to their own means to pay for legal counsel, expenses and, perhaps, a large damage award. The most common way to protect the Directors and Officers is through purchasing Directors and Officers Professional Liability Insurance. This

is especially true for Non-Profits that seek unpaid high visibility members and volunteers.

3. Officers also have the potential of being sued by **creditors** for statements made in financial documents. If the "deal" doesn't work for creditors, everything gets re-examined to determine who will be held accountable.

4. Differences of opinion often surface within **Boards of Directors**. When these differences break out of the boardroom as accusations or lawsuits, it can be very costly to the company, the directors, or the shareholders. Directors and officers often find themselves in a "darned if you do, darned if you don't" situation. Don't overlook the need for protection against claims from within your organization.

5. You may need other types of "**Professional Liability**" if the damage that you could cause doesn't result in "property damage" or "bodily injury" to someone. If the loss is only your customer's down time or a delay in getting to market, you may need an "**Errors and Omissions**" type of policy. Discuss these possibilities with your broker.

6. Work with an agent who is familiar with E&O concepts and can easily and thoroughly explain the difference between "**Occurrence**" and "**Claims Made**" types of policies There are many "fine points' to Professional Liability Insurance, aka Errors & Omissions Insurance, aka E&O. Don't assume it "responds" to claims and policy periods like General Liability. It usually does not. Most E&O policies require the loss to have occurred and the claim to be made during the same policy period or there is no coverage. This difficult condition can be changed by policy endorsements extending coverage

"backwards" to the start of other policy periods or "forwards" for a future time period. It will cost you, but it is usually the only way to stay protected.

7. Many E&O policies include the costs to administer and settle claims within the limits of coverage. This, of course, reduces the amount left for your protection. You usually can't change this feature of the policy, so be aware of it. You may need to purchase more insurance to provide for these expenses.

8. Many E&O policies let <u>you</u> decide whether to accept or reject a settlement offer. Common to policies that offer these options, is something aptly named a "**hammer clause**". It penalizes or "hammers" you if you do not accept a settlement offer and the judgement is greater than the insurance company settlement offer, by requiring you to pay a portion of the settlement amount in excess of the insurance company's offer. Other early settlement acceptance inducements may be available, as well.

Business Auto Insurance Don'ts and Do's

1. Like the Property Insurance, don't insure what you wouldn't claim. Parking lot dents, windshield cracks are maintenance costs, not insurance losses. Take a $500, $1,000 or even greater deductible and pocket the premium savings. And keep your claims history clean. You won't get a dollar for dollar reduction in premium, but if you constantly use the insurance policy as a maintenance program, the insurance company will recover their costs through your premium or they may decide they can do without it altogether.

2. Is buying the **damage waiver** from auto rental companies a good idea? We really don't know, but when you multiply the daily rate times 365 days in a year, it is really expensive!

   The difficulty in making this decision is that your broker rarely knows what the rental contract obliges you to do. That means your broker can't know the difference between what your policy will do (if it provides Hired Car Physical Damage at all) and what you are obligated to do under the rental contract.

One of my clients was invoiced $1,200 for damage "costs" and administrative fees that were not covered by his business auto policy. It's rare, but it was an unpleasant way to end a business trip.

The Hired Auto Physical Damage coverage in a Business Auto Policy should cover most, but probably not all, expenses if a rental car is damaged.

3. Is the additional cost of **the business auto enhancement endorsement** my insurance company offers a good buy? It's impossible to say without seeing the endorsement and knowing what you are trying to accomplish with your insurance program, but the answer is often "yes."

   The reasons for this are that these types of "bells & whistles" endorsements provide additional liability coverage while adding coverage like towing, rental, lease/loan gap. Spread out over the cost of insuring a fleet of vehicles, the additional cost is usually minimal.

4. Is **Lease Gap or Loan Gap** insurance a good buy? Sometimes, but only for the first year or two of a lease or loan. It is designed to pay the difference between what is owed on the finance agreement and the depreciated value (actual cash value) of the vehicle. It is in the first year or two that the "deal is upside down", which means that the car is worth less than the finance agreement. The Lease/Loan Gap provision would include the difference in the claim settlement.

5. Don't assume that trailers are covered by the insurance on the vehicle that pulls them. Rule of thumb: if it is over 1,000 pounds GCW (gross cargo weight), it needs to be listed in your policy vehicle schedule (NOT equipment schedule!) and needs to have coverage under the auto liability, not the general liability.

6. Don't insure your vehicles for all coverages if you are not using them. If a truck or trailer will not be used for an extended period of time (like winter), check into "**seasonal layup**" (removing all but comprehensive or "other than collision" physical damage coverage). Even better, ask your broker if the insurance company will offer a prospective credit based on expected layup time. This will give you the layup credit earlier and it will save a lot of administrative work taking off and putting on vehicle coverages. It should also help to prevent mistakes of not adding back needed coverage.

7. Why would you want to buy more than the **minimum limits** of liability insurance your state requires? You probably would never "want" to, but here are a couple of good reasons for buying more than your state requires:

First, you could easily become liable for more than your state minimum limits. Then your are insuring with your company's treasury (not a good idea).

Second, how you respond to a serious claim or lawsuit will impact your company's reputation, goodwill, and, possibly, the ability to remain in business.

Third, by purchasing greater limits of liability, you can usually purchase greater limits of underinsured and uninsured motorists bodily injury liability which is improved protection for yourself and your employees.

Fourth, remember that the opposing side in a lawsuit wants cash, not your business assets. Try to have enough to satisfy them…sometimes, the concept of insurance as "bait" succeeds.

8. Doesn't auto liability get really **expensive for greater limits**? Relatively speaking, no. It costs about 12% to 15% more to double your liability limits. Decreasing your protection, you save only 12% to 15% if you halve your protection.

9. Don't leave yourself exposed to employee lawsuits. Remove the **Fellow Employee Exclusion** so your policy, not your company, will pay if one employee sues another for bodily injury damage.

10. Don't assume your Business Auto Policy covers you outside of the United States of America. Most policies will extend to **Canada**. Most do not extend to **Mexico**. A few have very limited coverage in Mexico. That's it – no coverage anywhere else.

11. Don't assume your vehicles are rated properly by the insurance company. As you might expect, using them the least will cost you the least. For example, driving a truck a shorter distance (less than 50 miles one way) to a worksite and parking it all day, will produce a lower premium cost than driving it 200 miles each day. Generally, a smaller, lighter truck will cost less to insure than a larger, heavier truck of the same value.

12. Don't assume your **rating territory** is correct, either. Where your vehicles are "garaged" (kept at night or when not on the

road) is also a major factor. Check the territory code and ask what it means if you don't know.

13. Don't assume all insurance companies have the same **standards for drivers** or even make regular motor vehicle department checks on your drivers. It's better to maintain your own high standards and do regular driver checks. If you transfer too much risk or responsibility to the insurance company through poor driver selection, it will transfer too much premium expense right back to your company.

14. Equipment or accessories permanently installed on your vehicles should be noted to your insurance company and broker and included in the cost of the vehicle. This can be less costly than insuring them on an Equipment Floater or Inland Marine policy.

15. Truck **cargo** is not insured by your business auto policy. It is insured by the appropriate Inland Marine coverage such as Tools, Equipment, or Transportation. It may also be provided by a special property endorsement.

Inland Marine (Floaters) Insurance Don'ts and Do's

1. Most claim payments for **contractor's equipment and tools** and many other things insured by "equipment floaters" are on a **depreciated basis**. Many brokers waste their customers' money by listing items at new purchase price or replacement cost and never changing the values. That causes is higher premiums and unrealistic expectations.

2. Do keep your **equipment list** up-to-date and review it EVERY year with your broker. If your broker won't do that for you, change brokers.

3. Most insurance companies do <u>not</u> offer replacement cost policies for contractors equipment or tools, but some might offer "Functional Replacement cost" for some items, for a higher premium rate. It's not "new for old, like kind and quality," but a "similar condition" basis. Given the right circumstances, you could get a lot of value for relatively little premium increase.

4. Don't assume "**equipment**" is "equipment." With the redefining of "vehicle" or "auto" anything that is self-propelled or of a certain weight, may no longer have the correct coverage

if it is listed as "equipment" in an Inland Marine policy versus as an "auto" in a Business Auto policy. You need to ask your broker on this one.

5. "Inland Marine" or "Equipment Floater" is usually the section of an insurance policy that covers things that leave your premises. Don't assume that because you call it "property" is should be insured in the "Property Section" of your policy. Look at the definitions and discuss this with your broker. Most property definitions end coverage at less than 1,000 feet from your premises. Some policies are more expansive that others, but discussion is better than assumption.

6. On the other hand…Sometimes a property endorsement will offer a small amount of Inland Marine coverage. Don't assume that you must ALWAYS have an Inland Marine or Equipment Floater section. Ask your broker. This question could save you hundreds or even thousands of dollars by not requiring a separate Inland Marine section or policy.

7. Insurance coverage is usually very specific (sometimes too specific), including some causes of loss, excluding others. A "change in condition" is usually an Inland Marine type of coverage. Some causes of losses are Spoilage (usually food and other perishables), Contamination (such as mixing different types of plastic feedstocks), or even changes caused by dampness or temperature fluctuations. If it's a "weird" condition, it will usually be an Inland Marine risk.

8. Most EDP or Electronic Data Processing (**computer**) coverage is a type of Inland Marine insurance. Be careful, many look great, but don't provide protection for data recovery or laptops

off premises. Fewer address loss to smart phones or other newer types of handheld devices.

9. Don't assume your **"transportation insurance"** is correct. Most of what is given in the bells and whistles endorsements is protection only while the property is in or on an <u>owned vehicle</u>. It will not do a thing for you if you use any other class of vehicle such as common or contract carrier, delivery service, air freight, or ocean cargo.

10. Speaking of **"ocean cargo"** – don't assume anything! Read the coverage description. The better policy language is for "door to door" or from the factory in the far-off, foreign country, during transport to the shipyard, in the shipyard, on the ship, in the U.S. shipyard, during transport to your facility, until it is off-loaded or delivered to your premises. It should include any interim storage, or intermodal transport, too!

11. **"Air freight"** policies can have the same terminology and difficulties as ocean cargo.

12. Check for exclusions for **war or piracy** or certain areas of navigable waters in the "ocean cargo" policy, too. You could sail right into an exclusion…

Worker's Compensation Insurance Don'ts and Do's

1. It's the law, and you should do it. Actually, the law sometimes just requires you to provide the protection and it's up to you to decide how or if to insure. Most of the time, you should insure. If you don't, you are guaranteeing the benefits with your company treasury and <u>that</u> could be very expensive.

2. **Employee Classifications** are critical to the rate making process. Be certain your employees have not been assigned to a higher risk (more expensive) classification. You don't get more coverage by paying more premiums than required.

3. **Experience Modification Factors** or "Experience Mods" are a way to determine how effective you are at controlling claims costs. "Average" is 1.00; it's like getting a "C" on your report card. A lower number, like .90 or even .85, indicates that your claims are better than average; it's like getting a "B" or an "A". If the "mod" is a higher number, like 1.15 or 1.25 is like getting a "D" or an "F". Investigate the resources your insurance company offers to help you control the Experience Mod.

4. There are **auditing services** that will assist you in examining claims and resultant costs. The price paid for these outside services could be worth much more in premium savings if errors, miscalculations, or fraudulent claims are discovered and corrected. Your broker should be able to recommend a good audit service for you. You should interview the audit service and have a clear understanding of what they will do and what they will not do.

5. **Workers Compensation** is not General Liability coverage. There are separate policy sections or endorsements to provide this important coverage. Employer's Liability is sometimes added to General Liability sections, but it is really a Workers Compensation coverage.

6. Depending upon the laws of your state, **Employer's Liability** may or may not pay for damages. If not, the coverage is only for legal expenses. Your broker should know how "intentional tort" is handled in your state. Ask. It is a very important part of your overall protection.

Umbrella (Excess) Liability Insurance Don'ts and Do's

1. Don't assume "umbrellas" give protection in areas not covered by underlying liability policies (auto, general liability, employer liability, etc.). Often they are only "excess" or in addition to other existing liability coverage.

2. In addition, the umbrella liability policy usually covers only "bodily injury" or "property damage" type claims and not the professional or "wrongful act" type claims.

3. On occasion, you do receive protection for claims not covered by "**Underlying Coverage**" (such as Auto Liability, or General Liability). This shouldn't be relied on too much because the umbrella may change from policy period to policy period and you could lose protection you thought you had. Generally, if it is important enough to have the protection, it is important enough to have basic or underlying coverage for the risk, as well.

4. Umbrella policies are usually purchased in "units" or "**layers**" of millions of dollars such as a $1,000,000 Umbrella or a $25,000,000 Excess Liability Policy. You can also have

policies over or "excess of" other umbrella or excess policies. Such arrangements quickly become complicated, especially when the same insuring company is not used for all "layers" of coverage. This "layering" needs to be done very carefully.

5. Do buy the umbrella or excess policy from the same company that provides the underlying liability insurance whenever possible. There is much less chance for coverage gaps or unexpected retained amounts (differences between underlying insurance "stopping points" and excess insurance "starting points")

Claims Don'ts and Do's

1. A good claim adjuster (usually an insurance company employee, not a public adjuster or one hired on a fee basis) can actually find coverage for a loss than you might not have known existed. They are generally polite, professional people with a difficult job.

2. The claims adjuster cannot add coverage that is not in the policy, even if your broker told you it was covered. If it is covered, the insurance company will have put it in writing. No broker has the authority to change the policy. Only the insurance company can do that and they will do it in writing, with a policy amendment, frequently called an "endorsement."

3. It is to everyone's advantage to have the claim settled promptly and fairly. Difficulties arise when there is not a good record of what was lost, when it was lost or what caused it. Conflicts arise when expectations are not met. Experienced claims adjusters understand that there is usually an emotional component to every claim. They understand if you just need to "back away" from the situation for awhile. Unfortunately, they operate under state insurance laws so they have time and formality limitations and requirements, too. Do question. Do discuss. Don't threaten. Don't yell.

Bonds (Surety) Don'ts and Do's

1. Bonds are like getting a credit line from an insurance company and it takes a similar volume of paperwork, too. Allow one to three months to "set up a bond line."

2. Do have your financial paperwork in order. The procedure (underwriting) is much the same. The insurance company (surety) reviews your financials (personal and business), assets and liabilities, bank lines of credit, past, current and future activities. A good bond underwriter knows what to ask for and won't burden you with unnecessary requests. But they do need a **lot** of information.

3. Understand why you are requesting a bond. Businesses have different bonding needs and there are different types of bonds to fulfill these needs. Common bonds are license and permit (contractors), bid bonds (usually for government work, these prove you can get the next two types of bonds). Performance bonds are for work you say you will complete on time and supply bonds are for materials you say you will deliver on time.

Risk Management Don'ts and Do's

1. Establish goals. Realistic goals. You will have losses, insured and uninsured. Start with broad categories of concern, then fill in with the details.

2. Make a plan that is realistic. Not too elaborate, not to simple. One that can be followed and understood, yet addresses the changing needs of your company.

3. Follow the plan. If you don't, you will have wasted time and will not know what problems you are facing.

4. Review the results.

5. Adjust the plan. Then go at it again.

6. Alan Hill, CPA, CSA, Principal with Rea & Associates, Inc. recommends an annual review of your insurance, just like your taxes, business plans, or other important documents. He's correct. Everything changes so fast in the business world today. It's too easy for your insurance program to become an

afterthought and no longer consistent with the reality of your company.

7. Do plan NOW for a loss or claim. Who and how do you notify? What are the expected expenses? What are the procedures you have in place to show that you "have it under control" when the regulators or media show up? Consider the expense of a loss to your customers (they will expect you to pay). The expense to notify those affected. Comply with legal requirements (federal, state or local). The loss of reputation (how do you <u>really</u> feel about your company's goodwill?)? The loss of your customers' future business?

8. Do include business continuation planning in your disaster recovery program. There are many sources of information that you can access to begin to develop your company's program. This is one area that if <u>YOU </u>don't do it, it will NOT be done.

9. Don't rely on your "memory" to be able to recall what property is in your business. **Photograph it**. Don't video it. Photographic or "still" images are easier to reproduce into prints and then you will be able to draw and mark on them. Shelving, clocks, pictures or artwork on walls? Extra chairs and filing cabinets? Plants in the waiting area? Office supplies in storage closet? Extra tool boxes (with tools?), racks, equipment in warehouse? It can all be part of a claim, but you need to be able to remember it and document it in order to claim it.

10. **Thermographic surveys** are some of the hottest (pun intended) methods of detecting electrical problems before they become losses. Most of the time, the cost of the survey is less than your deductible. Or the deductible you <u>should</u> have.

About the Author

Rich Rozman, CLU, ChFC, works with manufacturing, processing, and contracting businesses. He brings 30+ years of experience from a wide variety of insurance industry segments that include property casualty insurance and loss control services, group benefits, and special financial services to his clients.

"Five Sources of Risk", "Five Broker Functions", and the "Five Point Always Guarantee" are his client-centric concepts developed to help his clients manage their risk and insurance programs.

He can be reached at:

Rich Rozman
P.O. Box 1776
Willoughby OH 44094-1776

Phone: 800-626-0435

Fax: 800-500-7650

or via email at:

rrozman@seibertkeck.com

www.ingramcontent.com/pod-product-compliance
Lightning Source LLC
Chambersburg PA
CBHW051241170526
45165CB00004B/1528